Anchors for Anxiety

A Stability Guide for Living With Anxiety Without Losing Yourself

Dr. Cindy H. Carr, D.Min. MACL

The Anchored Series

This book is published by **CHC Connect**.

Printed in the United States of America
First Edition, 2026

ISBN: 978-1-971192-27-7

For permissions or inquiries, contact:
Cindy H. Carr
cindyhcarr@outlook.com
www.cindyhcarr.com

About the Anchors Series

The Anchors series exists to help people live steady in the face of mental illness through practical tools, clear language, and compassionate support.

Each diagnosis-specific volume offers a structured set of Anchors (principles + practices) tailored to a particular struggle.

- *Anchors for Bipolar Disorder*
- *Anchors for Major Depressive Disorder*
- *Anchors for PTSD*
- *Anchors for Anxiety*
- *Anchors for ADHD*

Anchors of Support is written for the people who walk alongside someone living with mental illness—family, friends, ministry leaders, and helpers.

Anchors of Faith is the spiritual companion across the whole series. It is designed for readers who want to walk with God day-to-day while also taking mental health seriously as a real clinical reality.

Dedication

To the ones who live with a nervous system that sounds alarms too loudly—and who keep showing up anyway.

And to the people who stayed—steady, educated, and kind.

Table of Contents

How to Use This Book

1) Start with Chapters 1–4 to build your foundation: identity (you are not your anxiety), understanding the anxiety loop, building a support team, and learning to relate differently to anxious thoughts.

2) Chapters 5–8 focus on skill-building and practice: exposure/approach, treatment planning, nervous system anchors, and panic/physical anxiety tools.

3) Chapters 9–12 help you apply skills in real life domains (social life, relationships, work/school), and build relapse-prevention rhythms.

At the end of each chapter you will find an Anchor Check—short prompts to help you practice. You do not need to answer every prompt perfectly. Choose one next step and practice consistency.

If you are reading in a difficult season, you may not have the energy for long chapters. That's okay. Read one section. Write one sentence. Choose one action. Then return.

Chapter 1
You Are Not Your Anxiety

Anchor 1: Identity—
You are not your anxiety

Anchor statement: I am not my anxiety; anxiety is something I experience, not who I am.

Protects: Fusion with anxiety, shame-based identity, and hopelessness.

Why this matters in anxiety: When you treat anxiety as your identity, every symptom feels like a verdict. Separating "me" from "my anxiety" is the foundation for every skill that follows.

Anxiety can feel like a fact. It arrives with urgency, physical symptoms, and a storyline that sounds persuasive: "Something is wrong. Something bad is coming. You need to fix it right now." If you've lived with anxiety, you already know this voice can be loud—even when you're doing everything "right."

This chapter is your first Anchor: separating who you are from what anxiety does. You are not your anxiety. Anxiety is something your brain and body do—often in an attempt to protect you—and it is treatable.

What Anxiety Is (and Why It Feels So Real).

Clinically, anxiety disorders involve persistent fear or worry that is out of proportion to the actual situation and that interferes with daily life. The worry can be "in your head," but it also shows up in the body—restlessness, fatigue, muscle tension, stomach distress, irritability, sleep problems, and difficulty concentrating. (American Psychiatric Association, 2022).

Anxiety is not just a "thought problem." It's an alarm system problem. When your nervous system predicts danger, it mobilizes you to respond. That mobilization can feel like proof that danger is real—even when the threat is uncertain, exaggerated, or hypothetical.

Different anxiety disorders have different flavors (generalized anxiety, panic, social anxiety, phobias, and more), but they share a common loop: perceived threat → alarm response → avoidance or safety behavior → short-term relief → long-term reinforcement of fear. (American Psychiatric Association, 2022).

Normal Anxiety vs. an Anxiety Disorder

Anxiety itself is not the enemy. Some anxiety is normal and even helpful—like a smoke detector that alerts you to take action. The problem is when the detector becomes too sensitive, goes off too often, or stays on for too long.

A useful rule of thumb: anxiety becomes a disorder when it repeatedly drives impairment—when it shrinks your life. That might look like avoiding people, places, tasks, decisions, or emotions; spending hours in reassurance-seeking; or living with constant tension that disrupts sleep, health, work, or relationships. (National Institute for Health and Care Excellence, 2011).

What Anxiety Is Not

Anxiety is not your identity. It is not a character flaw, a moral failure, or a lack of faith. It is not proof that you are unsafe, unprepared, or incapable. Anxiety is a set of learned patterns in the brain and body—patterns that can be unlearned and replaced.

Anxiety also isn't a reliable prophet. It specializes in "what if," not "what is." It treats uncertainty like danger and urgency like wisdom. One of the biggest skills you'll build in this book is learning to slow down urgency so you can choose your next step on purpose.

How Anxiety Commonly Shows Up

Anxiety can be obvious—racing heart, sweating, trembling, panic. But it can also be quiet and strategic:

- Overthinking and mental replay (trying to solve feelings with analysis).
- Reassurance-seeking (from people, Google, checking, tests, "just to make sure").
- Avoidance (skipping events, delaying decisions, staying busy to outrun discomfort).
- Safety behaviors (always sitting near the exit, carrying "just in case" items, rehearsing scripts).
- Perfectionism and overpreparing (mistaking control for safety).
- Body scanning (monitoring sensations as if they are warnings).

These strategies often work in the short term—they reduce discomfort quickly. But they teach the brain a powerful lesson: "I survived because I avoided." That makes anxiety stronger over time.

A Quick Safety Note (Body First, Then Skills).

Anxiety can mimic medical problems, and medical problems can mimic anxiety. If your symptoms are new, sudden, severe, or paired with concerning physical signs (for example, chest pain, fainting, trouble breathing, or neurological symptoms), get medical evaluation. It is also worth discussing common contributors like sleep loss, thyroid issues, anemia, medication effects, substance use, and caffeine. (National Institute for Health and Care Excellence, 2011).

Make the Invisible Visible: Tracking Anxiety on Purpose

Anxiety lies about progress. On a hard day, it will tell you you're back at zero. Measurement-based care is a simple way to stay grounded in reality: track symptoms consistently so you can see patterns and trends.

One widely used tool is the GAD-7, a 7-item questionnaire that helps estimate anxiety severity and track change over time. It is not a label or a test of worth—it is data. Many clinicians use it weekly or every few weeks to guide care. (Spitzer et al., 2006).

The U.S. Preventive Services Task Force now recommends screening adults age 64 and under (including pregnant and postpartum persons) for anxiety disorders, with the important note that a positive screen must be followed by a fuller assessment and access to evidence-based care. (U.S. Preventive Services Task Force, 2023).

You are not alone in this. National survey data suggest that about 19% of U.S. adults experience an anxiety disorder in a given year. (National Institute of Mental Health, n.d.).

Anchor Preview: Support Is Part of Treatment

Building a support team early is not an optional add-on—it is part of treatment. Anxiety gets louder when you are alone with it. The right people help you reality-check, take the next step, and follow through on your plan. This book will help you choose your people, define roles, and make support specific (not vague).

The Anchor: Identity, "Me" vs. "My Anxiety"

Write two short lists. Keep it simple and honest.

1. ME:

    - What matters to me (values).
    - What I want my life to include (even with anxiety present).
    - How I want to treat myself and others when I'm stressed.
    -

2. MY ANXIETY:

    - What my anxiety predicts (its favorite "what ifs").
    - What my anxiety demands (urgency rules).
    - What my anxiety pushes me to do (avoid, check, reassure, overprepare).

Now add one sentence: "Even when anxiety shows up, I can choose to act like ME." This sentence is not denial. It's direction.

Anchor Check

- I can say, out loud, "I am not my anxiety."
- I can name at least two ways anxiety shows up for me (thoughts, body, behaviors).
- I understand the loop (threat → alarm → safety behavior → relief → reinforcement).
- I can identify one safety behavior I want to reduce this week.
- I will track anxiety at least once this week (GAD-7 or a simple 0–10 rating).

Chapter 2
Build Your Support Team

Anchor 2: Connection—
Build your support team

Why this chapter comes early

Most people try to "beat" anxiety alone. That makes sense: anxiety tells you to hide, to handle it quietly, to not be a burden.

But the same way anxiety thrives on secrecy and avoidance, recovery thrives on support, structure, and follow-through.

Building a support team early is not an optional add-on—it is part of treatment.

For anxiety, the logic is simple: the more activated your nervous system becomes, the harder it is to think clearly, make decisions, and stick with skills.

A support team helps you do three things when anxiety is loud: (National Institute for Health and Care Excellence, 2011) borrow calm and reality, (U.S. Preventive Services Task Force, 2023) take the next right step, and (National Institute for Health and Care Excellence, 2011) keep going long enough for the plan to work.

What we mean by a support team

A support team is a small circle of people and resources who help you move from "I'm trapped" to "I have a plan."

Your team can include professionals (primary care, therapist, psychiatrist), personal supports (partner, friend, family), and community supports (peer group, faith/community leaders, workplace/school supports).

Your team is not a jury evaluating your anxiety.

Your team is a scaffold—something you lean on while you build strength and skill.

Support is part of evidence-based care

Most modern anxiety guidelines are built around stepped care: start with the least intrusive effective intervention, then "step up" intensity when symptoms persist or impairment increases (National Institute for Health and Care Excellence, 2011).

Stepped care only works when you have follow-up, monitoring, and a plan for what happens next—meaning you need people involved (National Institute for Health and Care Excellence, 2011).

Shared decision making is the evidence-based way to do this: you and your clinicians (and, when you choose, your trusted supports) work together to choose a plan that fits your values, risks, and preferences (National Institute for Health and Care Excellence, 2011).

The goal is not to find the "perfect" plan. The goal is to choose a plan you can actually do.

When to build your team (hint: before the next flare).

If you wait until you're in a spike, you'll build your team from inside the panic.

That's like trying to install a seatbelt during a crash.

Build your team while you're relatively steady:

- When you can think two steps ahead.
- When you can write down what helps.
- When you can ask for support without apologizing for needing it.

Then, when anxiety spikes, your job is simple: follow the plan.

The core roles (and what each role is for).

1) Primary care clinician (or medical home).

Role: rule-outs, medication conversations, referrals, and continuity.

Anxiety often shows up in the body—sleep disruption, gastrointestinal distress, muscle tension, palpitations.

A primary care clinician can help you check medical contributors, review medications/substances that worsen anxiety, and coordinate next steps.

2) Therapist (skills + exposure support).

Role: build your skill set and help you practice what anxiety tells you to avoid.

For most anxiety presentations, cognitive behavioral therapy and exposure-based approaches are central tools.

A therapist also helps you build a relapse-prevention plan—what to do when symptoms return.

3) Medication prescriber (when needed).

Role: medication education, monitoring, and adjustments when symptoms are impairing or persistent.

Medication is not a "failure." It is one of several evidence-based options in stepped care (National Institute for Health and Care Excellence, 2011).

If you do use medication, the goal is not to erase every anxious feeling; the goal is to reduce symptom intensity so you can use skills and live your life.

4) One or two trusted people (your 'day-to-day anchors').

Role: reality checks, gentle accountability, and presence.

Choose people who can do these three things:

- stay calm (or at least not escalate),
- respect boundaries, and
- follow a plan rather than improvising.

You do not need a large team. You need a reliable one.

5) Community supports (optional but powerful).

Role: belonging and repetition.

Peer support groups, group therapy, faith/community leaders, or recovery communities can normalize your experience and reduce isolation.

They also help you practice sharing your story without shame.

Choose wisely: helpful support vs. anxious support

Not everyone who loves you is automatically helpful for anxiety recovery.

Some people accidentally reinforce anxiety by rescuing, reassuring, or helping you avoid triggers.

That can feel good in the moment—and keep anxiety strong long-term.

Look for supporters who can:

- validate your feelings without feeding the fear,
- remind you of your plan,
- encourage gradual approach rather than avoidance,
- and stay connected even when you're uncomfortable.

Scripts: how to ask for support without overexplaining

Use short, direct requests. Anxiety will try to make you justify your need. You don't have to.

Script A (general):

"Hey—anxiety's been spiking. I'm working a plan. Can I loop you in as one of my supports?"

Script B (what you need in the moment):

"I don't need reassurance. I need you to help me stick to my plan. Can you stay with me for 10 minutes while I do the next step?"

Script C (when you need help getting care):

"I think I need a professional evaluation. Can you help me make the appointment and follow through?"

Script D (boundaries):

"I'm not looking for advice right now. What helps most is calm presence and reminding me of the plan."

Boundaries that protect recovery

Support is not the same as rescuing.

Rescuing looks like: repeated reassurance, doing the hard thing for you, making big decisions during spikes, or helping you avoid triggers every time.

Support looks like: calm presence, coaching you back to skills, helping you take one step, and following up later.

Two boundary questions:

1) "Does this help me approach life, or does it help me avoid life?"

2) "Will future-me be stronger because of what I'm doing right now?"

Your team plan (one page).

Write this down and share it with your core supports.

A) My early warning signs:

• (Example) sleep changes, irritability, constant checking, increased avoidance, more reassurance seeking

B) My top 3 skills that help:

• (Example) paced breathing, brief exposure step, grounding + movement

C) What helps from my supports:

• (Example) "sit with me," "remind me of the plan," "help me schedule the appointment," "walk with me"

D) What does NOT help:

• (Example) debating fears, reassurance loops, last-minute cancellations, pressure to "just relax"

E) When to escalate care:

• If symptoms are worsening for 2–4 weeks despite practice

• If avoidance is shrinking life (work/school/relationships).

• If panic or distress becomes unmanageable

• If there is any self-harm risk or inability to care for basic needs (seek urgent help) (National Institute for Health and Care Excellence, 2011).

Follow-up: how your team keeps the plan alive

A plan that isn't reviewed becomes a wish.

Set a simple cadence:

- Weekly (or biweekly) check-in with a trusted person: "What's one win? What's one next step?"

- Regular clinical follow-ups when starting or changing treatment.

- Routine outcome tracking when possible—so you can see trends, not just feelings (National Institute for Health and Care Excellence, 2011).

The U.S. Preventive Services Task Force notes that screening only helps when people who screen positive are evaluated and connected to evidence-based care (U.S. Preventive Services Task Force, 2023).

Your support team helps make that connection real.

Anchor Plan: Build Your Support Plan (This Week).

Choose 2–3 people for specific roles (check-in, exposure support, logistics). Share your one-sentence spike plan and one boundary you want them to hold.

Anchor Check

1) Who are 2 people you can ask to be "day-to-day anchors"? Write their names.

2) What is one specific job each person can do that supports recovery (not reassurance)?

3) What is one boundary you need to say out loud?

4) What is one appointment or next step you will schedule this week?

5) What is your one-sentence plan for a spike? (Example: "Pause, breathe, name the fear, do the next step, text my anchor.").

Chapter 3
Understand the Anxiety Loop

Anchor 3: Awareness—
Understand the anxiety loop

In Chapter 1, we separated you from your anxiety. In Chapter 2, we built a support team so you are not fighting alone. Now we zoom in on the engine that keeps anxiety running: the anxiety loop. Most anxiety disorders—worry, panic, social anxiety, phobias—are maintained by a similar set of steps: threat interpretation, body alarm, and behaviors that bring short-term relief but long-term stuckness.

This chapter is not here to make you "think your way out" of anxiety. It is here to help you map the pattern so you can practice new responses with your support team and your skills toolkit. Evidence-based care for anxiety commonly includes cognitive behavioral approaches and exposure-based methods, which target this loop directly (Salkovskis, 1991; Clark, 1986).

The Anxiety Loop (The 6 Steps).

You can think of anxiety like a smoke alarm. A good smoke alarm is sensitive. A too-sensitive smoke alarm goes off when you make toast. Anxiety disorders are often like a smoke alarm that's firing too often, too intensely, or in the wrong situations. The loop below explains why the alarm keeps getting re-triggered.

1) Trigger: A situation, sensation, thought, memory, or uncertainty shows up.

2) Threat story: Your brain assigns meaning: "This is dangerous," "I can't handle this," or "Something bad is about to happen."

3) Body alarm: Adrenaline and stress responses rise (heart rate, tension, dizziness, nausea, urge to escape).

4) Urge: A powerful push to do something right now—avoid, escape, check, reassure, control, or numb.

5) Safety behaviors: You do something that lowers anxiety quickly (avoidance, reassurance, compulsive checking, over-preparing, carrying "just in case" items, distraction).

6) Short-term relief → long-term learning: Relief arrives, and your brain learns: "Good thing I escaped/checked/controlled—danger was real." The loop strengthens.

The cruel trick is step 6: the relief feels like proof. But relief is not proof. Relief is what nervous systems do when the threat signal drops.

Avoidance and Safety Behaviors: The Fuel That Keeps Anxiety Going

Avoidance is any move that prevents you from fully meeting the feared situation, sensation, or uncertainty. Safety behaviors are the subtler cousins of avoidance—things you do in the feared situation to feel safer, so you never learn that you can handle it without the safety behavior. Researchers have argued that safety-seeking behaviors can prevent "disconfirmation" of threat beliefs and maintain anxiety. (Salkovskis, 1991).

Common forms of avoidance:

- Not going (canceling, staying home, leaving early).
- Not starting (procrastinating, delaying until it feels "perfect").
- Not feeling (numbing with substances, screens, or constant busyness).
- Not risking (never speaking up, never trying, never being seen).

Common safety behaviors (often mistaken for "coping"):

- Reassurance: repeatedly asking others or searching online for certainty.

- Checking: pulse, breathing, doors, messages, mistakes, "Did I offend them?"
- Over-preparing: scripts, excessive research, rehearsing every scenario.
- Carrying safety items: medications "just in case," water, charms, specific routes, sitting near exits.
- Avoiding eye contact, speaking quietly, hiding in groups, using your phone to escape.
- Compensating: perfectionism, people-pleasing, controlling every variable.

Important: We are not calling you "weak" for using safety behaviors. Safety behaviors are intelligent attempts to survive. They just become expensive over time—shrinking your life while anxiety grows.

Three Common Anxiety Loops (So You Can Recognize Yours).

1) The Worry Loop (often seen in generalized anxiety).

Trigger: uncertainty (money, health, relationships). Threat story: "If I don't worry, I'll be unprepared." Body alarm: tension and restlessness. Safety behavior: endless problem-solving, reassurance seeking, mental reviewing. Relief: temporary sense of control. Long-term cost: more worry, less trust in your ability to handle uncertainty.

2) The Panic Loop (often seen in panic disorder).

Trigger: a normal body sensation (heart racing, dizziness). Threat story: "I'm dying," "I'll faint," "I'll lose control." Body alarm increases. Safety behavior: escape, checking, avoiding exertion, carrying rescue items. Relief: the wave passes. Long-term cost: stronger fear of sensations and more avoidance. Cognitive models highlight catastrophic misinterpretations of bodily sensations as a maintaining factor. (Clark, 1986).

3) The Social Threat Loop (often seen in social anxiety).

Trigger: being observed. Threat story: "They'll see I'm anxious," "I'll be judged." Body alarm: blushing, trembling, mind blank. Safety behavior: rehearsing, hiding, over-explaining, avoiding eye contact, leaving early. Relief: you get through it. Long-term cost: social situations keep feeling dangerous, confidence doesn't get to grow.

Where We Interrupt the Loop

You do not need to stop anxiety from showing up. You need to change what happens after it shows up. There are three leverage points:

Leverage Point 1: Name the threat story—Anxiety speaks in predictions, not facts. Label it: "My anxiety is predicting ______."

Leverage Point 2: Reduce safety behaviors gradually—Not all at once. We taper them so your nervous system can learn.

Leverage Point 3: Practice approach (exposure)—Approach teaches your brain new learning: "I can be with this and be okay." Modern exposure work often emphasizes inhibitory learning and expectancy violation rather than waiting for fear to disappear (Clark, 1986).

This is why anxiety treatment often focuses less on "calming down" and more on "learning through doing."1–3 Calm can be a byproduct. Learning is the target.

Anchor Exercise: Map Your Loop (10 minutes).

Use the template once this week. Do it after an anxious moment, not during your highest panic. If you can't write, voice-note it.

Trigger (what happened?)	
Threat story (what did anxiety predict?)	
Body alarm (what did you feel?)	
Urge (what did you want to do?)	
Safety behaviors (what did you do to reduce anxiety?)	
Short-term relief (what changed right away?)	
Long-term cost (what did it teach your brain?)	

Bring this map to your support team (Chapter 2). The goal is not shame. The goal is clarity.

Anchor Plan: One Small Loop-Interrupt (This Week).

Pick ONE safety behavior to reduce by 10–20% this week. Examples:

- If you Google symptoms for 30 minutes, set a timer for 25.
- If you check your phone for reassurance 20 times, aim for 18.
- If you sit by the exit every time, choose the second-closest seat once.
- If you avoid the task, do 5 minutes of "approach" and stop (approach practice counts).

Tell your support person your plan. Ask them for one role: accountability, encouragement, or accompaniment.

Anchor Check

- I can describe the 6-step anxiety loop in my own words.
- I can name at least 3 safety behaviors I use (including subtle ones).
- I mapped one recent anxious moment using the loop template.
- I chose one small safety behavior to taper this week (10–20%).
- I told someone on my support team what I'm practicing.

Chapter 4
Thoughts Are Not Facts and Uncertainty is Not Danger

Anchor 4: Anchoring to Reality—
Thoughts Are Not Facts

In Chapter 3 we mapped the anxiety loop and saw the moment it tightens: the threat story. Chapter 4 teaches you how to work with that story. Evidence-based approaches for anxiety often include cognitive-behavioral strategies that help you test anxious predictions, reduce catastrophic interpretations, and practice more flexible thinking—especially when paired with behavioral experiments and exposure (Dugas & Robichaud, 2007).

Important: This chapter is not a command to "think positive." It's a skill for distinguishing possibility from probability, and uncertainty from emergency. You can respect your mind without obeying it.

Your Brain Is a Prediction Machine

Your brain's job is not to make you happy—it is to keep you alive. When your threat system is sensitive, your mind generates rapid predictions: "What if…?" Anxiety is often the mind's attempt to reduce uncertainty. The problem is that anxiety treats uncertainty as if it were danger.

Most anxious thoughts fall into one of these categories:

- Catastrophe: “If this happens, it will be unbearable.”
- Overestimation of threat: “This is very likely.”
- Underestimation of coping: “I won’t be able to handle it.”
- Intolerance of uncertainty: “I must know for sure right now.”
- Over-responsibility: “If something goes wrong, it will be my fault.”

Common Anxiety Thinking Traps

Thinking traps are patterns—not character flaws. The goal is not perfection. The goal is awareness and choice.

Mind reading: Assuming you know what others think: “They think I’m awkward.”

Fortune telling: Predicting the future as if it’s already decided: “I’m going to panic.”

Catastrophizing: Jumping to the worst-case conclusion: "This will ruin everything."

All-or-nothing thinking: Only extremes count: "If I'm anxious, I failed."

Emotional reasoning: "I feel afraid, therefore it must be dangerous."

Safety math: Believing you can prevent bad outcomes by checking/controlling perfectly.

Notice how many traps end with urgency. Anxiety loves speed. Skill loves pause.

Anchor Exercise: The 5-Column Thought Record (15 minutes).

Do this after an anxious moment, not in the middle of your highest peak. Keep it short. You are training a new reflex.

1) Situation (facts only)	
2) Automatic thought / prediction	
3) Emotion + intensity (0–100)	
4) Evidence for / evidence against	
5) Balanced thought (realistic, not positive)	
6) Next right step (action)	

Tip: If you get stuck on a balanced thought, borrow this template: "It's possible that ______. It's also possible that ______. Right now, the best step is ______."

Behavioral Experiments: Testing Anxiety's Predictions

Anxiety argues in your head. Behavioral experiments answer in the real world. A behavioral experiment is a planned test of a prediction. It is not about proving you are safe forever—it is about gathering data.

How to run an experiment:

- Write the prediction: "If I ______, then ______ will happen."
- Rate belief (0-100).
- Choose a small test (10–20% stretch).
- Drop one safety behavior during the test (or reduce it slightly).
- Record what happened and what you learned.
- Re-rate belief (0).

Examples of experiments:

- Social anxiety: "If I pause before answering, they'll think I'm stupid." Test: pause for 2 seconds once.
- Health anxiety: "If I don't check my pulse, I'll miss a crisis." Test: delay checking by 10 minutes.

- Worry: "If I don't worry, I'll be unprepared." Test: schedule 10 minutes of worry time later; return to the present now.

The Uncertainty Skill: Trading Certainty-Seeking for Confidence-Building

Most anxiety disorders involve a struggle with uncertainty. Certainty-seeking (reassurance, checking, mental reviewing) feels helpful, but it teaches your brain that uncertainty is intolerable. Treatment often aims to build tolerance for uncertainty and confidence in coping. (Dugas & Robichaud, 2007).

Two phrases to practice:

- "I can't know for sure right now—and I can still choose my next step."
- "My goal is not certainty. My goal is capacity."

Use Your Support Team (Chapter 2) With This Skill

Ask a support person to play one of these roles:

- Mirror: repeat your prediction back to you in neutral language ("Your anxiety is predicting ______.").

- Coach: help you fill in the 5-column thought record (especially columns 4–6).
- Experiment buddy: accompany you during one small behavioral experiment.
- Boundary helper: help you reduce reassurance cycles kindly ("I love you. I can't answer that again, but I can sit with you.").

Anchor Plan: One Thought + One Test (This Week).

This week, choose ONE anxious thought you hear often and do TWO things:

- Write it down and label it (Anchor 1).
- Complete one short thought record (Anchors 1–3).
- Run one behavioral experiment that reduces ONE safety behavior by 10–20%.

Anchor Check

- I can label an anxious thought as a prediction (not a fact).
- I can name at least 3 thinking traps that show up for me.

Chapter 5
Approach Over Avoidance: Exposure, Practice, and New Learning

Anchor 5: Approach—
Move toward what you fear

"Moving toward feared situations weakens anxiety more than avoidance ever can."

In Chapters 3 and 4 we mapped the anxiety loop and learned how to respond differently to anxiety's threat story. Now we move into the most life-changing step for many people: approach practice—also called exposure. Exposure-based treatment is a core component of evidence-based care for many anxiety disorders (Salkovskis, 1991; Barlow, 2002; Abramowitz, 2006).

Exposure does not mean throwing yourself into your biggest fear with no support. Exposure means choosing a careful, repeatable practice plan that teaches your brain new learning: "I can handle this," "I can tolerate uncertainty," and "I don't need my safety behaviors to survive."2,3

What Exposure Is (and What It Is Not).

Exposure is planned, repeated contact with a feared situation, sensation, memory, or uncertainty—without using the usual avoidance or safety behaviors. It is the opposite of avoidance training.

Exposure is NOT:

- Not punishment. You are not "forcing" yourself to suffer.
- Not reckless. You do not skip safety, medical advice, or common sense.
- Not a promise that fear disappears. The goal is learning, not zero anxiety.
- Not done alone if you need support. Your support team (Chapter 2) matters.

Exposure IS:

- A way to retrain the brain's threat system through experience.
- A way to weaken avoidance and safety behaviors that maintain anxiety. (Salkovskis, 1991).
- A way to build confidence by proving you can cope—imperfectly, humanly, consistently.

Why Exposure Works: New Learning Beats Old Fear

Older explanations of exposure focused on "habituation" (fear goes down with time). Habituation can happen—and it's nice when it does. But modern exposure work emphasizes learning: your brain forms new memories that compete with the old fear memory (Barlow, 2002). This is sometimes called an inhibitory learning approach.

Your practice goal becomes: increase what you learn, not just decrease what you feel. That means you may finish an exposure still anxious—but wiser, freer, and more capable.

Key learning targets during exposure:

- Expectancy violation: "I predicted ______. What actually happened was ______."2,3
- Uncertainty tolerance: "I can't know for sure—and I can still do this."
- Safety behavior reduction: "I can be here without my usual crutches."5
- Self-efficacy: "I can cope with discomfort and keep going."

Four Types of Exposure (So You Can Choose the Right Kind).

1) Situational exposure: Approaching places, tasks, or situations you avoid (driving, stores, meetings, calls, elevators).

2) Interoceptive exposure: Practicing feared body sensations safely (e.g., spinning to feel dizziness) often used for panic. (Barlow, 2002).

3) Imaginal exposure: Working with feared images or memories when you can't do real-life exposure yet (or when the fear is about "what if").

4) Response prevention (ERP-style): Approaching triggers while not performing compulsive or safety behaviors that reduce anxiety short-term (commonly used in OCD-related patterns). (Abramowitz, 2006).

You don't have to pick one type forever. Many plans mix types over time. If you have trauma history, talk with a qualified clinician about pacing and the safest approach.

Anchor Exercise: Build Your Exposure Ladder (Your Courage Plan).

An exposure ladder is a list of approach steps from easier to harder. You start where you can succeed (a stretch, not a snap), then build.

Step 1: Choose one fear domain.

Pick ONE domain to start (you can build more ladders later): social, panic sensations, health worries, leaving home, driving, contamination, work performance, etc.

Step 2: List 10–15 approach steps.

Include small steps. Small steps are not "cheating." Small steps are training.

Step 3: Rate each step (0–10).

0 = no anxiety, 10 = highest anxiety. You're looking for steps in the 3–7 range to start.

Step 4: Choose a safety behavior to reduce.

Pick ONE safety behavior to taper during practice (checking, reassurance, escape routes, over-preparing). Reducing safety behaviors is often the difference between "getting through it" and learning from it. (Salkovskis, 1991).

Exposure Step	Anxiety Rating (0–10)	Safety Behavior to Reduce	What I Learned (after practice)

Tip: If you struggle to list steps, ask your support person to brainstorm with you and remind you of small wins you've already made.

How to Run an Exposure (A Simple Script).

Before:

- Name the prediction: "My anxiety predicts ______."
- Set the goal: "My goal is learning, not comfort."2,3
- Pick your safety-behavior reduction: "Today I will not ______ (or I will reduce it by 10–20%)."5
- Decide duration and repetition (e.g., 10–20 minutes, 3–5 times per week).

During:

- Stay with the experience long enough to learn something new (not necessarily until anxiety is gone).
- Notice urges to escape/check/reassure. Label them as urges, not commands.
- Use simple grounding (slow exhale, feet on floor) without using it as a "get rid of anxiety" button.

After:

- Write the data: What did I predict? What happened? What did I learn?
- Rate belief change (0): "I believed the danger story at ____%. Now I believe it at ____%."

- Choose the next step (same step again, or one notch higher).

Repeat is the magic word. One exposure is helpful. Repeated exposure is rewiring.

Common Exposure Problems (and How to Fix Them).

Problem: I'm doing exposures but not improving.

Fix: Check safety behaviors. If you are still heavily checking/reassuring/escaping, your brain may not be getting new learning. Reduce one safety behavior by 10–20%. (Salkovskis, 1991).

Problem: I start too hard and burn out.

Fix: Start smaller. Success builds success. Use a 3–6 rating step first.

Problem: I use exposures to prove I'll be safe forever.

Fix: Shift goal: tolerate uncertainty, build coping confidence, learn flexible responses (Barlow, 2002).

Problem: I feel shame for being anxious during practice.

Fix: Exposure is not a performance. Anxiety is expected. Courage is continuing with anxiety present.

Use Your Support Team for Exposure (Chapter 2).

Support people can help without becoming your safety behavior. Here are healthy roles:

- Coach: helps you plan exposures and celebrate effort, not perfection.
- Buddy: accompanies you for early steps (then gradually fades support).
- Accountability partner: checks in on your practice schedule.
- Boundary helper: refuses reassurance loops while offering presence ("I'm here with you, but I won't answer that again.").

If your support person becomes your main safety behavior, your plan can stall. The goal is growth toward independence.

Anchor Plan: Two Practices This Week

- Build one exposure ladder with at least 10 steps.
- Complete TWO exposures from steps rated 3–7.
- Record one sentence of learning after each practice.

Anchor Check

- I can explain why exposure works (learning, not just habituation).
- I can name at least 2 avoidance or safety behaviors that maintain my anxiety.
- I built an exposure ladder with at least 10 steps.
- I completed two approach practices this week.
- I recorded what I learned and chose a next step.

Exposure changes anxiety through experience, not insight—and that's why it works. But you don't have to do it alone, and you don't have to "DIY" your way through something that's genuinely hard. If you've been practicing and still feel stuck, overwhelmed, or unsure how to structure your next steps, support can be the difference between trying harder and getting better. In the next chapter, we'll talk about treatment anchors—how to choose the right level of care, what evidence-based therapy looks like, and when medication or higher support makes sense.

Chapter 6
Seeking Treatment is Wisdom

Anchor 6: Treatment—
Use evidence-based care wisely

Start With the Right Level of Care (Stepped Care).

Think of anxiety care like a staircase. Some people do well with self-guided skills and periodic support. Others need structured therapy. Some need medication support. And some need higher-intensity services when symptoms are severe or safety is at risk. Guidelines commonly recommend a stepped-care model: begin with the least intensive evidence-based option that is likely to help, then step up if improvement is not happening (Clark, 1986; Conrad & Roth, 2007; Trauer et al., 2015).

Step 1: Foundations: Education, self-guided skills (this book), sleep and substance basics, support team check-ins.

Step 2: Structured psychotherapy: CBT/exposure-based therapy, ACT, group therapy, brief interventions in primary care.

Step 3: Medication and combined care: SSRIs/SNRIs (and other options when appropriate) often alongside therapy.

Step 4: Higher-intensity services: Intensive outpatient programs (IOP), partial hospitalization (PHP), specialty clinics, crisis services when needed.

Stepping up is not failure. It is wisdom. You wouldn't treat a broken bone with positive thinking. Anxiety deserves the same respect.

Therapy Anchors: What Works (and Why).

The strongest evidence base across many anxiety disorders supports cognitive-behavioral approaches, including exposure-based methods (Conrad & Roth, 2007; Trauer et al., 2015; Baldwin et al., 2011). Different therapy styles may share common ingredients: skill-building, practice between sessions, and changing avoidance patterns.

Evidence-based therapy options you may encounter:

Cognitive Behavioral Therapy (CBT): Targets thinking traps and behavior patterns; often includes behavioral experiments and exposure (Baldwin et al., 2011).

Exposure-based therapy: Approach practice designed to create new learning (Chapter 5).

Acceptance and Commitment Therapy (ACT): Builds psychological flexibility: making room for anxiety while moving toward values. (Hayes et al., 2012).

Mindfulness-based approaches: Train attention and decentering; often used as an adjunct to CBT/ACT. (Bernstein et al., 2015).

Group therapy: Can be effective and cost-efficient; adds practice and accountability (Clark, 1986).

A practical rule: choose a therapist who talks about a plan, practice, and measurable goals—not just insight. Good therapy is compassionate and active.

How to Choose a Therapist (Quick Checklist).

- They can name the approach they use (CBT, exposure/ERP, ACT, etc.) and explain why it fits your symptoms.
- They measure progress (a tool like GAD-7, panic rating, or functional goals) and adjust the plan if you're stuck.
- They assign practice between sessions (behavioral experiments, exposure ladder steps, thought work).
- They talk about safety behaviors and avoidance (Chapter 3) and how to reduce them gradually.

Medication Anchors: What to Know Before You Decide

Medication can be a useful support for anxiety—especially when symptoms are persistent, disabling, or not improving with skills and therapy alone. For many anxiety disorders, first-line pharmacologic options often include SSRIs and SNRIs (Clark, 1986; Conrad & Roth, 2007; Trauer et al., 2015),11 Medication is not a personality change. It's one tool to reduce symptom intensity so you can do the learning work.

Common medication categories (plain-language overview):

SSRIs: Often first-line for generalized anxiety, panic, social anxiety, and related conditions; may take several weeks to help (Clark, 1986; Conrad & Roth, 2007; Trauer et al., 2015),11

SNRIs: Also commonly used first-line in several anxiety disorders (Clark, 1986; Conrad & Roth, 2007; Trauer et al., 2015),11

Buspirone: Sometimes used for generalized anxiety; tends to be non-sedating, requires consistent dosing. (Baldwin et al., 2011).

Pregabalin: Included in some guidelines as an option for generalized anxiety in certain contexts. (National Institute for Health and Care Excellence, 2011).

Beta blockers: Sometimes used for performance-related physical symptoms (e.g., tremor); not a core treatment for generalized anxiety. (Baldwin et al., 2011).

Benzodiazepines: Can reduce anxiety quickly, but carry risks (dependence, tolerance, sedation). Usually reserved for short-term or specific situations and should be used carefully under medical guidance (Clark, 1986; Conrad & Roth, 2007; Trauer et al., 2015),11

If you have a history of substance use, are pregnant, have medical conditions, or take other medications, medication decisions deserve extra care and professional input.

If You Start Medication: A Supportive, Practical Framework

Many people stop medication early because they were not prepared for normal early bumps. Here are common best-practice themes to discuss with your prescriber (not one-size-fits-all). (Baldwin et al., 2011).

- Start low, go slow (especially if you're sensitive to side effects).
- Expect a delay: benefits often take weeks, not days.
- Plan for follow-up: schedule check-ins to adjust dose or switch if needed.
- Track symptoms weekly (e.g., GAD-7) so decisions are data-driven, not mood-driven.
- Do not stop suddenly without medical advice—some medications require tapering.

Ask directly: "What side effects should I watch for? What is the plan if this doesn't work? What's the timeline for reassessment?"

Why Therapy + Medication Can Be Powerful Together

For some people, medication lowers symptom intensity enough to fully engage in therapy and exposure practice. For others, therapy alone is sufficient. For many, the best plan changes over time. Collaborative care models in primary care—where a team supports medication management and brief psychotherapy—have demonstrated effectiveness for common mental health conditions, including anxiety

When to Step Up: Signs You Need More Support

Stepping up is about function and safety. Consider higher-intensity help if any of these are true:

- You are unable to complete daily responsibilities (work, school, caregiving) for weeks at a time.
- Avoidance is rapidly shrinking your life (leaving home, driving, eating, sleeping).
- Panic attacks or anxiety symptoms are frequent and feel unmanageable.
- You are using alcohol, cannabis, or other substances to cope most days.
- You have thoughts of harming yourself, or you feel unsafe. (Seek immediate help—call emergency services or a crisis line in your region.).

If you are in immediate danger or feel you might act on suicidal thoughts, seek urgent care right away. You deserve rapid support.

Anchor Exercise: Build Your Treatment Plan (One Page).

Use this page to clarify your plan. Bring it to your doctor, therapist, or support person.

My main anxiety patterns (worry/panic/social/avoidance)	
My biggest functional impact (what anxiety is taking from me)	
My current supports (people + services)	
Skills I'm practicing (from Chapters 3–5)	
Therapy plan (who/when/approach)	
Medication plan (if applicable) + follow-up date	
Step-up plan (what we do if I'm not improving)	

Share your plan with your support team. Ask one person to help you follow through—especially scheduling and follow-up.

Anchor Check

- I can describe stepped care and when to step up.
- I can name at least two evidence-based therapy approaches for anxiety.
- I understand first-line medication categories and key questions to ask a prescriber.
- I completed a one-page treatment plan I can share with professionals/supports.
- I chose one concrete next step for professional support.

Chapter 7
Understanding the Effect Anxiety Has on the Body

Anchor 7: Body—
Nervous system support matters

"Anxiety is not just in the mind; it is also in the nervous system and body."

What's Happening in Your Body During Anxiety

- Shortness of breath, sighing, chest tightness
- Dizziness, lightheadedness
- Stomach upset, nausea, diarrhea
- Muscle tension, jaw clenching, headaches
- Trembling, sweating, hot/cold flashes
- Restlessness, feeling "wired," difficulty sleeping

A key idea: body sensations are not proof of danger. They are signals of activation. When you interpret activation as catastrophe, the loop intensifies (Chapter 3). (Clark, 1986).

Regulation vs. Reassurance: The Calm Trap

Regulation skills are helpful when they help you stay in the moment and keep doing what matters. They become unhelpful when they become a rule: "I must calm down before I can live."

Signs a regulation tool is becoming a safety behavior:

- You use it urgently to make anxiety disappear immediately.
- You stop the task or leave the situation unless the tool "works."
- You repeat the tool over and over to get certainty.
- You judge yourself as failing if you still feel anxious afterward.

If you recognize these patterns, don't panic. Just shift your goal statement to: "I'm using this to support my body while I continue my approach practice."

Why this matters in anxiety: When your body is activated, your mind is more likely to interpret sensations as danger. Supporting your body helps you stay present while you practice approach (not avoidance).

Practice 7.1: The Longer Exhale

Breathing is one of the fastest ways to influence your nervous system. Slow breathing—especially with a longer exhale—can increase parasympathetic activity and reduce arousal (5) You are not trying to force calm; you are creating a steadier platform.

Practice (2 minutes):

- Inhale gently through the nose for ~4 seconds.
- Exhale slowly for ~6 seconds (as if fogging a mirror softly).
- Repeat 10 cycles. Keep shoulders relaxed.
- If 4/6 is too much, use any ratio where the exhale is longer than the inhale.

Use this before exposures, during stressful moments, or after. If you start to chase calm, shorten the practice and return to your task.

Practice 7.2: Grounding Through the Senses (30–60 seconds).

Grounding brings your attention out of catastrophic prediction and back into the present. It's not denial; it's orientation.

- Name 5 things you can see.
- Name 4 things you can feel (feet, chair, fabric).
- Name 3 things you can hear.
- Name 2 things you can smell.
- Name 1 thing you can taste (or one thing you appreciate in this moment).

This is especially useful when your mind is spiraling. Then return to the next right step (Chapter 4).

Practice 7.3: Release the Grip (Tension Reset).

Anxiety often shows up as chronic muscle tension. Brief muscle relaxation can reduce physical strain and signal safety to your nervous system. (Conrad & Roth, 2007).

Practice (90 seconds):

- Press your feet into the floor for 5 seconds, then release.
- Squeeze your fists for 5 seconds, then release.
- Lift shoulders toward ears for 5 seconds, then drop.
- Unclench jaw; let tongue rest gently; soften forehead.

If you have trauma history, keep this gentle. You are aiming for "more ease," not perfect relaxation.

Practice 7.4: Movement as Nervous System Medicine

Regular physical activity reduces anxiety symptoms for many people and improves sleep, mood, and stress tolerance (9) Movement also teaches your body: "Activation does not equal danger," which can be especially helpful for panic-related fears.

Two simple movement prescriptions:

- 10-minute walk most days (start where you are).
- 2 days/week of light strength work (push, pull, squat, carry) with safe guidance.

If movement triggers fear of sensations, use it as a gentle interoceptive exposure (Chapter 5) and practice "I can feel this and be okay."

Practice 7.5: Sleep as Stabilizer

Sleep and anxiety affect each other. Poor sleep increases reactivity; high anxiety disrupts sleep. Cognitive behavioral therapy for insomnia (CBT-I) is an evidence-based approach for improving sleep. (Trauer et al., 2015).

Three sleep anchors:

- Regular wake time (even after a bad night).
- A 30-minute wind-down routine (dim lights, low stimulation).
- If you can't sleep after ~20 minutes, get up briefly and do something quiet until sleepy.

If you suspect sleep apnea, restless legs, or another medical sleep condition, consult a clinician. Treating sleep disorders can significantly improve anxiety.

Practice 7.6: Caffeine, Alcohol, Cannabis, and the Anxiety System

Substances can change anxiety in the short term and the long term. Caffeine can increase jitters and panic-like sensations in sensitive people (Klevebrant & Frick, 2022). Alcohol can temporarily numb anxiety but often worsens anxiety and sleep later (a rebound effect) (Roehrs & Roth, 2001). Cannabis affects people differently; for some it increases anxiety or panic (Kedzior & Laeber, 2014).

Supportive questions (not shame):

- What is my nervous system paying for this coping strategy later?
- What happens to my sleep when I use it?

- Is my use increasing avoidance (not feeling, not facing)?

Practice 7.7: Fuel and Blood Sugar Stability

Skipping meals, dehydration, and blood sugar swings can mimic anxiety sensations (shakiness, dizziness, irritability). A simple anchor: eat something with protein and fiber within a few hours of waking, and hydrate across the day.

Anchor Exercise: Your Nervous System Menu (Pick 3).

Choose three body practices you can realistically do this week. Put them on a "menu," not a rigid rule.

Body Anchor (choose 3)	When I'll use it
Longer exhale breathing	
Senses grounding	
Tension reset	
Movement	
Sleep anchor	

Write a reminder at the top of your menu: "These are supports, not escape routes."

Anchor Plan: Regulation + Approach

This week, do both:

- Practice two body practices on 4 days (even when you're not highly anxious).
- Complete one approach practice (Chapter 5).
- Use one body practice before or after the exposure—not to avoid it.

Anchor Check

- I can explain the difference between regulation and reassurance.
- I practiced the longer-exhale breath at least 3 times.
- I used grounding once and returned to my next right step.
- I chose movement or sleep as a stabilizer this week.
- I completed one approach practice without turning calm into a compulsion.

Chapter 8
Panic and Physical Anxiety: When Your Body Feels Like the Emergency

Anchor 8: Presence—
Stay engaged without needing to be calm

If you have ever felt your heart race, your breath tighten, dizziness rise, and a wave of fear slam into you, you are not alone. Panic and high physical anxiety can feel like a medical crisis. Many people think, "I'm having a heart attack," "I'm going to faint," or "I'm losing control." The good news: panic follows a predictable loop—and there are evidence-based ways to break it. (National Institute for Health and Care Excellence, 2011; American Psychiatric Association, 2022; Clark, 1986; Barlow, 2002).

This chapter helps you (1) understand what panic is, distinguish panic from situations that require medical attention, reduce catastrophic interpretations of body sensations, and (4) practice interoceptive exposure—learning to tolerate the sensations that anxiety uses to scare you. (National Institute for Health and Care Excellence, 2011; American Psychiatric Association, 2022; Clark, 1986; Barlow, 2002).

What Panic Is

A panic attack is a sudden surge of intense fear or discomfort accompanied by physical symptoms (like palpitations, shortness of breath, chest tightness, shaking, nausea, chills, or feeling unreal). Panic is a false alarm—your body's threat system firing when there is no immediate external danger.

Panic becomes a disorder when people begin to fear the panic itself and change their life to prevent it. Avoidance, checking, and safety behaviors then maintain the loop (Chapter 3) (National Institute for Health and Care Excellence, 2011; American Psychiatric Association, 2022; Clark, 1986).

The Panic Loop (Why It Keeps Coming Back).

Cognitive models of panic emphasize a key mechanism: catastrophic misinterpretation of bodily sensations (Clark, 1986). A normal sensation (heart rate increase, lightheadedness) is interpreted as danger, which increases fear, which increases sensations. Soon you're trapped in a feedback loop.

Trigger: A sensation (caffeine, stress, exertion, a skipped meal) or a situation (crowded store, driving).

Catastrophic interpretation: "This means I'm dying/fainting/going crazy." (Clark, 1986).

Anxiety surge: Fear rises, adrenaline spikes, breathing changes.

More sensations: More dizziness, chest tightness, tingling, shaking.

Safety behavior: Escape, sit down, check pulse, call someone, avoid exertion.

Relief: The wave passes; brain learns safety behavior 'worked,' strengthening fear of sensations.

The goal is not to eliminate sensations forever. The goal is to stop treating sensations as proof of catastrophe.

Panic vs. Medical Emergency: A Responsible Boundary

Most panic sensations are not dangerous, but some physical symptoms can signal a medical issue. This book cannot diagnose you. If you have new, severe, or unusual symptoms—especially chest pain with exertion, fainting, severe shortness of breath, or symptoms with neurological changes—seek medical evaluation. If you are unsure, it is appropriate to get checked. (National Institute for Health and Care Excellence, 2011).

Many people find it helpful to get one thorough medical evaluation if panic symptoms are new. Then, once urgent causes are ruled out, they can treat panic as panic and practice the skills below.

Three Panic Practices

Practice 8.1: Interoceptive Exposure (Training With Sensations).

Interoceptive exposure means intentionally creating safe body sensations you fear—so your brain learns they are tolerable. It is a core component of CBT for panic (Barlow, 2002; Clark, 1986).

Safety note:

If you have significant heart or lung disease, are pregnant, have uncontrolled blood pressure, or have another medical condition, talk with a clinician before doing interoceptive exercises.

Choose ONE exercise to start (repeat 3–5 times/week):

Dizziness practice: Spin in a chair for 30 seconds or turn in place, then sit and observe sensations without checking.

Breathlessness practice: Jog in place for 60 seconds or climb stairs, then stand and let the sensations rise and fall.

Tingling practice: Hyperventilate gently for 30 seconds (ONLY if advised appropriate), then practice slow exhale recovery.

Heat practice: Hold a warm mug or do a brief brisk walk, notice heat and sweating without alarm.

Heart-rate practice: Do 20 jumping jacks; then sit and practice "I can feel this and be okay."

During the practice, your goal is to stay present without the usual safety behavior (checking, escaping, calling for reassurance). After the practice, write: "I predicted ______. What happened was ______. What I learned was ______."

If a Panic Attack Hits: A 5-Minute Script

- 1) Label: "This is panic. My body is activated."
- 2) Exhale long: 10 slow breaths (exhale longer than inhale).
- 3) Drop the struggle: "I can allow this wave."
- 4) Stay: remain where you are if it's safe; reduce one safety behavior by 10–20%.
- 5) Reorient: name 5 things you see; return to the next right step.

This script is not magic. It's practice. Each time you respond without escape, you teach your brain that panic is survivable.

Common Panic Myths (Reality Anchors).

Myth: Panic will last forever.

Reality: Panic peaks and passes. Waves feel endless, but they end. (National Institute for Health and Care Excellence, 2011).

Myth: If my heart races, I'm dying.

Reality: Increased heart rate is a normal activation response; panic itself is not a heart attack. (Still get medical evaluation if symptoms are new or concerning.).

Myth: If I feel unreal, I'm going crazy.

Reality: Derealization/depersonalization can occur in high anxiety and are not psychosis. (American Psychiatric Association, 2022).

Myth: I must avoid triggers to be safe.

Reality: Avoidance teaches your brain the triggers are dangerous; approach practice retrains the alarm (5).

Use Your Support Team for Panic (Chapter 2).

Panic often recruits reassurance. Support can be helpful without feeding the loop.

- Coach language: "I believe you. This is panic. Let's breathe and stay."
- Boundary: refuse repeated reassurance questions; offer presence instead.
- Exposure partner: accompany you for early interoceptive or situational exposures (then fade support).
- After-action review: help you write the learning sentence after an episode.

Anchor Plan: Sensation Practice + One Approach Step

- Do interoceptive exposure 3 times this week (same exercise).
- Reduce one safety behavior during practice (10–20%).
- Do one situational exposure that you typically avoid because of panic fear (rated 3–7 on your ladder).
- Write one learning sentence after each practice.

Anchor Check

- I can explain the panic loop (catastrophic interpretation → more sensations → more fear).
- I know the safety boundary for seeking medical evaluation when symptoms are new or concerning.
- I practiced one interoceptive exposure exercise at least twice.
- I reduced one safety behavior during panic/sensation practice.
- I wrote what I learned instead of only tracking how anxious I felt.

Chapter 9
Being Seen is Not danger

Anchor 9: Being Seen—
Visibility is survivable. You can be seen and still be safe.

Social anxiety can make ordinary moments feel dangerous: speaking up in a meeting, ordering food, making eye contact, dating, presentations, even answering the phone. It is not vanity—it is a threat response tied to judgment, rejection, or embarrassment. The good news: social anxiety follows the same anxiety loop (Chapter 3) and responds well to evidence-based treatment—especially cognitive-behavioral approaches and exposure-based practice (Clark & Wells, 1995; Salkovskis, 1991).

In this chapter, you will learn:

- how social anxiety maintains itself (Clark & Wells, 1995).
- how self-focused attention and safety behaviors keep fear alive (Salkovskis, 1991).
- how to run social exposures and behavioral experiments.
- how to build connection without turning people into reassurance machines.

What Social Anxiety Is (and Why It Feels So Personal).

Social anxiety disorder involves persistent fear of social or performance situations in which you may be scrutinized or negatively evaluated. People often fear embarrassment, rejection, or being perceived as incompetent, weird, or unlikeable (Clark & Wells, 1995). Because humans are wired for belonging, social threat can register as survival threat.

You may notice anxiety before, during, and after social situations. Social anxiety often includes post-event rumination—replaying what you said and searching for mistakes. (Clark & Wells, 1995).

The Social Anxiety Loop

Social anxiety is maintained by a predictable pattern: anticipation, self-focused attention, safety behaviors, and post-event review. Cognitive models emphasize that people shift attention inward (monitoring symptoms and performance) and use safety behaviors that prevent disconfirmation of feared beliefs

1) Trigger: A social situation (meeting, party, phone call, dating, classroom).

2) Threat story: “They will judge me,” “I’ll say something stupid,” “They’ll see I’m anxious.”

3) Self-focused attention: You monitor your face, voice, hands, mind, and try to control symptoms.

4) Safety behaviors: Rehearsing, avoiding eye contact, speaking less, over-explaining, holding your breath, using your phone, staying on the edge of the group.

5) Short-term relief: You survive the situation; anxiety drops afterward.

6) Long-term learning: Brain concludes: "Good thing I hid/controlled/escaped—danger was real."

7) Post-event rumination: You replay the event, magnify flaws, and strengthen fear for next time.

The loop is brutal because it tricks you into believing your safety behaviors are the reason you weren't rejected. But what if the real reason is that you are human—and most people are not grading you the way your anxiety is?

Reality Anchor: The Spotlight Effect

Anxiety convinces you that everyone is watching you. Social psychology research suggests people often overestimate how much others notice their appearance and behavior (sometimes called the "spotlight effect") (Gilovich et al., 2000). This does not mean people never judge—only that anxiety inflates the spotlight.

Common Social Safety Behaviors (What to Taper).

In social anxiety, safety behaviors often look like "good manners," "being prepared," or "being quiet." The key question is: do they reduce anxiety short-term but shrink your life long-term?

- Over-rehearsing what you will say; scripting entire conversations.
- Avoiding eye contact or speaking very softly.
- Holding your breath, tensing muscles, trying to hide shaking.
- Over-explaining, apologizing, filling silence immediately.
- Staying near exits; arriving late; leaving early.
- Using your phone as a shield.
- Avoiding disagreement; people-pleasing to prevent rejection.

Your job is not to eliminate all preparation or politeness. Your job is to reduce the behaviors that function as "armor," so you can learn you are safe enough without them

Anchor Skill: Shift Attention Outward

Social anxiety pulls attention inward: "How do I look? How do I sound?" But inward monitoring amplifies symptoms and self-criticism. Evidence-based CBT protocols often teach shifting attention outward to the environment and the other person

Two outward-attention practices:

- Name 3 details you can see in the room (colors, shapes, objects).
- During conversation, listen for 2 pieces of information about the other person (not about your performance).

A connecting question can become an anchor: "What is it like to be you right now?" (Ask internally, not aloud.).

Behavioral Experiments: Testing Social Predictions

Social anxiety predictions tend to be specific: "They'll think I'm boring," "I will blush and they'll reject me," "If there's silence, I will fail." Behavioral experiments test these predictions in real life (Chapter 4).

Experiment templates:

- Prediction: "If I ______, then ______ will happen."
- Safety behavior to reduce: "I will not ______ (or I will reduce it by 10–20%)."
- Data: "What actually happened?"
- Learning: "What did I learn about my ability to cope? About other people?"

Examples of small experiments:

- Allow 2 seconds of silence before responding once.
- Ask one simple question in a meeting.
- Make one brief eye contact moment and smile.
- Say "I'm not sure" without over-explaining.
- Share a minor preference ("I'd prefer Thai tonight") without apologizing.

Anchor Exercise: Build a Social Exposure Ladder

Use the ladder from Chapter 5 but tailor it to social fear. Include steps that train being seen, not just being present.

Why this matters in anxiety: Support works best when it builds capability. Boundaries replace certainty-giving with presence, coaching, and approach practice.

Social Exposure Step	Anxiety Rating (0–10)	Safety Behavior to Reduce	Learning (after practice)

After the Social Moment: Stop the Replay Loop

Post-event rumination is like watching a highlight reel of your 'worst' moments on repeat. It strengthens fear (Clark & Wells, 1995). Instead, practice a brief review that is data-based and time-limited.

The 3-minute review:

1) What did I do that was courageous (even small)?

2) What did I learn about my predictions vs reality?

3) What is my next practice step?

Then stop. If your brain demands more review, label it: "My anxiety is trying to keep me safe by replaying." Return to your life.

Connection Without Reassurance Traps

It is healthy to want support. The trap is turning people into certainty dispensers: "Did I seem weird?" "Are you mad?" "Did I embarrass myself?" Repeated reassurance can become a safety behavior that keeps anxiety alive (Chapter 3). (Salkovskis, 1991).

Try these replacement requests:

- Instead of "Did I do okay?" → "Can you sit with me while my anxiety settles?"
- Instead of "Was it awkward?" → "Can you help me name what I learned?"
- Instead of "Do they like me?" → "Can you help me plan my next exposure step?"

Use Your Support Team (Chapter 2) for Social Anxiety

- Practice partner: role-play one conversation opener for 2 minutes, then stop (no endless rehearsal).
- Exposure buddy: accompany you to an early social step, then fade support over time.
- Coach: help you taper one social safety behavior.
- Reality mirror: remind you of the spotlight effect and reframe post-event rumination into learning.

Anchor Plan: Two Being-Seen Practices

- Create a social exposure ladder with at least 10 steps.
- Complete TWO steps rated 3–7 this week.
- Reduce ONE social safety behavior by 10–20% during each practice.

Anchor Check

- I can describe the social anxiety loop (self-focus → safety behaviors → rumination).
- I identified at least 3 social safety behaviors I use.
- I practiced shifting attention outward once in a conversation.
- I completed two social exposure practices and recorded what I learned.
- I used the 3-minute review instead of spiraling in replay.

Chapter 10
Relationship and Family Anchors: Boundaries, Reassurance Cycles, and Repair

Anchor 10: Boundaries—
Presence helps; certainty fuels.

Anxiety is personal, but it is not private. It can shape how you ask for help, how you avoid conflict, how you seek reassurance, and how you interpret other people's moods. Partners, parents, children, friends, and coworkers often become part of the anxiety loop without intending to—especially through accommodation and reassurance (Linehan, 2015). This chapter teaches you how to build relational support that strengthens recovery rather than feeding anxiety.

In this chapter, you'll learn:

- what anxiety accommodation is (Linehan, 2015).
- how reassurance loops form.
- how to set kind boundaries.
- how to communicate needs clearly.

When Love Becomes a Safety Behavior: Anxiety Accommodation

Anxiety accommodation means other people change their behavior to help you avoid distress—repeatedly. Common examples include answering the same reassurance questions, checking things for you, enabling avoidance, changing plans to prevent anxiety spikes, or acting as your constant "proof" that everything is okay. Accommodation is usually motivated by compassion, but research suggests it can maintain anxiety over time by reinforcing avoidance and dependence (Linehan, 2015).

Common accommodation patterns:

- **Reassurance on repeat:** "Are you sure?" "Are you mad?" "Did I offend them?"
- **Doing the feared thing for you:** making calls, driving, ordering, speaking up.
- **Changing routines to prevent triggers:** routes, seating, leaving early, avoiding events.
- **Checking/monitoring:** symptoms, locks, messages, news, weather, health stats.
- **Relationship over-functioning:** partner becomes manager/therapist instead of partner.

Important: We are not blaming anyone. Accommodation is what families do when they are scared for someone they love. This chapter is about adjusting the pattern so support builds capability instead of dependence.

The Reassurance Cycle (Why It Never Feels Like Enough).

Reassurance offers quick relief. But quick relief can become a training signal: "I can't tolerate uncertainty unless someone else reduces it." Over time, reassurance must increase to produce the same relief (a tolerance effect). Then both people feel trapped.

Reassurance cycle map:

- Trigger → anxious thought ("Something is wrong").
- Reassurance request ("Tell me it's okay").
- Temporary relief.
- Uncertainty returns (often within minutes or hours).
- Stronger reassurance request.
- Relationship strain (frustration, resentment, guilt).

The goal is not to remove comfort from relationships. The goal is to replace certainty-giving with courage-building.

Boundary Anchors: Kind Limits That Protect Love and Progress

A boundary is not a punishment. A boundary is a clear statement of what you will do and what you won't do—so the relationship stays healthy. Boundaries help both the anxious person and the support person avoid burnout and resentment. (Linehan, 2015).

Three boundary principles:

- Be warm and firm: kindness + consistency.
- Name the goal: "I'm doing this because I love you and I want anxiety to have less power."
- Offer presence instead of certainty: support feelings without feeding the loop.

Boundary scripts (support person):

- "I love you. I'm not going to answer that question again, but I can sit with you while the feeling passes."

- “I can’t check that for you. I believe you can handle the uncertainty. Let’s do one step from your plan.”
- “I hear your anxiety. I’m willing to help you practice, not to help anxiety win.”
- “I’m here. Let’s label the prediction and choose the next right step.”

Boundary scripts (you):

- “I want to ask for reassurance, but I’m going to try tolerating this for 10 minutes first.”
- “Can you help me do an exposure step instead of answering the question?”
- “Please don’t check for me. Please remind me of my plan.”
- “I’m feeling anxious and I need connection, not certainty.”

Relationship Anchors: Communication, Conflict, and Repair

Anxiety can distort communication. It can push you to demand immediate certainty, or to avoid expressing needs altogether. Healthy support is specific. It tells people what role you want them to play (Chapter 2).

Try this 4-part request:
1) **Name the moment:** "I'm feeling anxious right now."
2) **Name the need:** "I need connection / grounding / encouragement."
3) **Name the helpful action:** "Can you sit with me for 10 minutes?" or "Can you walk with me while I do this exposure?"
4) **Name the boundary:** "Please don't reassure me or answer the same question—help me practice instead."

Conflict Anchors: Anxiety, Anger, and Avoidance

Many people with anxiety avoid conflict because disagreement feels like danger. Others become irritable because chronic activation lowers patience. Avoiding conflict can protect you short-term, but it can damage relationships long-term.

Two skills for conflict:

- **Approach the conversation in small steps** (exposure principle). Start with a 5-minute check-in.
- **Use "I" statements and stay in the present:** "I felt ______ when ______. What I need is ______."

If conflict becomes unsafe (emotional abuse, threats, violence), seek professional help and safety planning.

Repair Anchors: Rebuilding Trust After Anxiety Has Taken Space

Anxiety can lead to missed plans, irritability, withdrawal, and broken promises. Repair is a skill. It includes acknowledging impact, naming the plan, and inviting collaboration.

A simple repair script:

- "I'm sorry for ______." (name impact, not excuses).
- "Anxiety has been loud, but I'm working on it."
- "Here's what I'm practicing (one sentence)."
- "Here's how you can help (one role)."
- "Here's the boundary we're using to stop reassurance loops."
- "Thank you for being here with me."

Anchor Exercise: Your Relationship Support Plan (One Page).

Use this plan with a partner/family member/friend. The goal is teamwork.

- My top 3 reassurance questions (what anxiety asks)
- My top 3 safety behaviors that involve others
- One boundary we will use (warm + firm)
- What my support person WILL do (presence, coaching, exposure buddy)
- What my support person will NOT do (repeat reassurance, check for me)
- How we will handle conflict (5-minute approach check-in)
- How we will repair after hard moments

If possible, review this plan weekly for a month. Adjust gently. Celebrate effort.

Anchor Plan: One Boundary + One Connection Practice

Choose ONE reassurance boundary to practice this week (10–20% reduction).

Tell your support person exactly what to do instead (presence, coaching, exposure buddy).

Have ONE 10-minute connection check-in that is not about anxiety (walk, coffee, shared activity).

Anchor Check

- I can explain how accommodation and reassurance can maintain anxiety.
- I identified one reassurance loop in a relationship.
- I practiced a boundary script (warm + firm).
- I completed a one-page relationship support plan with someone.
- I practiced one connection moment that is not focused on anxiety.

Closing reminder: Presence helps. Certainty fuels.

My top 3 reassurance questions (what anxiety asks)	
My top 3 safety behaviors that involve others	
One boundary we will use (warm + firm)	
What my support person WILL do (presence, coaching, exposure buddy)	
What my support person will NOT do (repeat reassurance, check for me)	
How we will handle conflict (5-minute approach check-in)	
How we will repair after hard moments	

Chapter 11
Work, School, and Performance: Anxiety, Perfectionism, and Getting Unstuck

Anchor 11: Consistency—
Small practice beats intensity

For many people, anxiety shows up most loudly in performance spaces: work, school, parenting tasks, deadlines, grades, money, leadership, and public evaluation. It can look like procrastination, over-preparing, re-checking, avoiding feedback, people-pleasing, or pushing so hard you burn out. These patterns are not laziness—they are often fear-based safety behaviors (Hayes et al., 2012; Martell et al., 2010).

This chapter will help you map performance anxiety through the anxiety loop (Chapter 3), challenge perfectionistic rules (Chapter 4), and build a plan for behavioral activation and approach practice (Chapters 5 and 7) so your life can move forward even with anxiety present.

The Performance Anxiety Loop

Performance anxiety often follows this pattern: high standards + fear of failure → avoidance or over-control → short-term relief → long-term stuckness. Perfectionism can function as a safety behavior: "If I do it perfectly, nothing bad will happen." But perfectionism usually increases anxiety over time and can impair performance and well-being (Hayes et al., 2012).

Trigger: A task with evaluation: an email, exam, presentation, performance review, assignment, application.

Threat story: "If I fail, I'm not safe," "If I make a mistake, I'll be judged," "I must get this right."

Body alarm: Tension, racing thoughts, restlessness, dread.

Safety behaviors: Procrastination, over-researching, rewriting, checking, asking for reassurance, avoiding feedback.

Short-term relief: Avoidance reduces anxiety now.

Long-term cost: Deadlines tighten, stress increases, confidence shrinks, and avoidance becomes the habit.

The main trap: anxiety convinces you that you need certainty or perfection before you can begin.

Perfectionism as a Rulebook (and Why It Backfires).

Perfectionism is often a set of rigid rules: "I must not make mistakes," "I must please everyone," "I must feel confident before I act." These rules are understandable attempts to avoid shame or rejection. But research suggests perfectionism is associated with anxiety, depression, burnout, and poorer well-being (Hayes et al., 2012).

Common perfectionistic rules:

- "If I can't do it perfectly, I shouldn't do it."
- "If someone is disappointed, I failed."
- "I must respond immediately or I'm irresponsible."
- "I must not look anxious."
- "My worth depends on my performance."

Reality anchor: competence is built through imperfect repetitions. Perfection is not a requirement for progress.

Values Anchor: What Matters More Than Anxiety?

Performance spaces trigger anxiety because they matter. Values help you aim. Instead of asking, "How do I stop feeling anxious?" ask, "What kind of person do I want to be in this situation?" ACT and related approaches emphasize moving toward values even when uncomfortable. (Hayes et al., 2012).

Values prompts:

- If anxiety were quieter, what would I do more of?
- What would 'courage' look like in my work/school this week?
- What does 'good enough' look like when I'm acting from values?

Getting Unstuck: The 10-Minute Start

When anxiety makes a task feel impossible, shrink the task. The goal is to begin, not to finish. Behavioral activation principles show that action can precede motivation; you don't have to wait to feel ready. (Martell et al., 2010).

Core Anchor 11—Consistency

"Small, repeated practice over time changes anxiety more than intensity ever will."

Protects: All-or-nothing bursts, burnout, discouragement after setbacks, relapse through loss of practice.

Why this matters in anxiety: Anxiety change comes from repetition: exposures, support, and body basics maintained over time. Returning after setbacks is the skill.

The 10-minute start script:

1) Name the task (one sentence).

2) Identify the smallest next action (open document, write one bullet, send one email draft).

3) Set a timer for 10 minutes.

4) Reduce one safety behavior (no rechecking, no tab-switching, no reassurance).

5) Stop at 10 minutes or continue if you want—either way, you win.

Anxiety hates small starts because small starts create momentum.

Attention Anchors: Managing Anxiety-Driven Distraction

Anxiety often hijacks attention: doom-scrolling, checking messages, scanning for mistakes, or "researching" endlessly. Attention anchors help you return to one next step.

Two simple attention anchors:

- Single-tab rule: one task, one tab for 10–25 minutes.
- Scheduled worry/review time: set a daily 10-minute window for worry or checking; outside that window, return to the task (Chapter 4).

These are not productivity hacks for perfectionism. They are exposure practices for uncertainty and 'unfinishedness.'

Mistakes and Feedback: The Exposure You Didn't Know You Needed

If you fear being judged, feedback can feel threatening. But feedback is how you grow. A powerful exposure is allowing small imperfections and tolerating the feeling of being evaluated

Two exposure practices for work/school:

- Send a message with one minor imperfection (no re-reading 5 times).
- Ask one clarifying question in a meeting or class (practice being seen).

Safety note: choose imperfections that are safe and appropriate—this is practice, not sabotage.

Burnout Anchor: Rest Is Part of the Plan

Anxiety and perfectionism can drive overwork. Over time, overwork increases anxiety, irritability, sleep disruption, and physical symptoms. If you are exhausted, your nervous system becomes more reactive. Body anchors (Chapter 7) are performance anchors too.

Two burnout boundaries:

- A hard stop time most nights (even if it's not perfect).
- One recovery ritual daily (walk, shower, stretching, prayer/meditation, music).

Anchor Exercise: Your Performance Practice Plan (One Page).

Use this page for ONE current task or goal.

Task/goal (one sentence)	
Anxiety prediction (what fear says)	
Perfection rule (the rigid rule)	
Balanced rule (realistic standard)	
Smallest next action (10-minute start)	
Safety behavior to reduce (10–20%)	
Exposure step (being seen / uncertainty)	
Support role (who will help + how)	

Bring this plan to a therapist, coach, or support person if you have one. If not, use your support team from Chapter 2.

Anchor Plan: Progress Over Perfection (This Week).

Pick ONE task you've been avoiding.

Do a 10-minute start on 3 days this week.

Reduce one safety behavior each time (checking, rewriting, reassurance).

Do one 'being seen' exposure (ask, share, submit, speak) and tolerate the discomfort.

Anchor Check

- I can map my performance anxiety through the anxiety loop.
- I can name one perfectionistic rule that drives my avoidance.
- I completed at least one 10-minute start.
- I reduced one safety behavior while working.
- I practiced one 'being seen' exposure and recorded what I learned.

Consistency: Small, repeated practice over time changes anxiety more than intensity ever will.

Chapter 12
Relapse Prevention, Setbacks, and Building A Life Bigger Than Anxiety

Anchor 12: Maintenance—
Return to your anchors after setbacks; maintenance is success.

If you have made progress, you may fear losing it. If you are still struggling, you may fear you'll be stuck forever. Chapter 12 is here to anchor you: change is built through repetition, support, and returning after setbacks. In anxiety recovery, skills are not "one-and-done." They are maintenance practices—like brushing your teeth or strength training.

This chapter helps you build a relapse-prevention plan: recognizing early warning signs, maintaining approach practice, handling setbacks with compassion, and strengthening the life domains that keep anxiety from becoming the center of everything (Hayes et al., 2012).

What 'Relapse' Often Looks Like in Anxiety

In anxiety, setbacks often show up as a quiet return of avoidance and safety behaviors—not as a dramatic breakdown. It might look like canceling plans again, checking more, reassurance seeking, procrastinating, or shrinking your world.

Common relapse signals:

- Avoidance is increasing (you're doing less, leaving earlier, staying closer to home).
- Safety behaviors are increasing (checking, reassurance, researching, controlling).
- Your anxiety "rules" return: "I must feel calm before I go."
- Sleep is worsening and recovery time after stress is longer.
- You are withdrawing from people or meaningful activities.
- You stop practicing exposures and skills because you feel "busy" or "fine."

Notice: these are behavior changes. Anxiety recovery is maintained by behavior—especially approach practice (Chapter 5).

The Maintenance Triangle: Approach, Support, and Body Basics

Most people stay well by maintaining three pillars:

1) Approach practice: You keep doing small exposures so avoidance does not re-grow

2) Support and accountability: You stay connected to people who encourage practice (Chapter 2).

3) Body basics: Sleep, movement, and substance boundaries (Chapter 7).

If one pillar weakens, the others matter even more. If all three weaken at the same time, relapse risk increases.

Setbacks Are Data, Not Verdicts

A setback can be triggered by life stress, illness, loss, transitions, conflict, or simply nervous system fatigue. The question is not "Why am I anxious again?" The question is: "What is my next right step?"

A compassionate reset script:

- Name it: "I'm having a flare-up."
- Normalize: "This is what anxiety does under stress."
- Return to one pillar today (approach, support, or body basics).
- Choose one small step (10–20% stretch).

Anchor Exercise: Your Relapse Prevention Plan (One Page).

Fill this out now—before you need it. Share it with at least one person on your support team.

My early warning signs (top 5)	
My top 3 safety behaviors that creep back	
My biggest avoidance pattern	
My 3 maintenance exposures (easy, repeatable)	
My body basics (sleep/movement/substance anchors)	
My support check-in plan (who/when/how)	
My professional plan (therapist/doctor; when to re-engage)	
My step-up plan (what I do if I'm not improving)	
My reminder to myself (one sentence)	

Maintenance exposures are not dramatic. They are small reps that keep your nervous system trained. Examples: one short phone call, one drive route, one social check-in, one uncertainty practice.

Schedule Maintenance Like a Prescription

The most common relapse reason is not loss of knowledge—it's loss of practice. Your brain returns to what it rehearses

Two scheduling options:

- Option A: Weekly exposure appointment (20–30 minutes). Put it on your calendar.
- Option B: Daily micro-exposure (5–10 minutes) tied to an existing habit (after coffee, after lunch).

If you wait to feel motivated, anxiety wins. Schedule beats mood.

Build a Life Bigger Than Anxiety

Anxiety shrinks your world. Recovery expands it. A strong relapse-prevention plan includes meaning: relationships, purpose, creativity, service, faith, play, rest. Values-based living helps anxiety take its rightful size—one part of a full life. (Hayes et al., 2012).

Values inventory (choose 2 to strengthen this month):

- Relationships (one weekly connection ritual).
- Health (movement or sleep anchor).
- Growth (learning, skill-building, education).
- Work/service (one meaningful contribution).
- Creativity/play (a hobby without performance pressure).
- Faith/spirituality (practice that grounds you).
- Rest (a protected recovery window).

When to Seek More Help (Again).

It is wise to step up support early. Consider re-engaging therapy or medical support if:

- Avoidance is increasing week to week.
- Panic or symptoms are frequent and feel unmanageable.
- You are relying on substances to cope most days.
- Sleep is severely disrupted for more than two weeks.

- You are not improving despite returning to practice.
- You have thoughts of harming yourself or feel unsafe (seek immediate help).

If you are in immediate danger or feel you might act on suicidal thoughts, seek urgent help right away. You deserve rapid support.

The 24-Hour Rule: Don't Let Anxiety Steal Two Days

A practical relapse-prevention anchor: if you avoid something today, do one small approach step within 24 hours. This keeps avoidance from becoming a new habit.

Anchor Plan: Your Maintenance Week

- Complete your one-page relapse prevention plan and share it with one support person.
- Schedule one maintenance exposure appointment on your calendar.
- Choose one body anchor to practice on 4 days (sleep or movement counts).
- Do one values-based action that has nothing to do with anxiety.

Anchor Check

- I can name my early warning signs of relapse.
- I know my top safety behaviors and avoidance patterns.
- I built a maintenance plan (exposure + support + body basics).
- I scheduled practice instead of waiting for motivation.
- I chose one values-based action that expands my life.

Safety Plan Worksheet

My warning signs (what I notice first)	
My internal coping steps (what I can do on my own)	
Places that help me feel safer (where I can go)	
People I can contact (names + numbers)	
Professional supports (therapist/doctor + contact)	
Crisis supports (local emergency / crisis line)	
How I want others to help me (what is helpful)	
What is NOT helpful (what makes it worse)	
Steps to reduce risk (remove/secure	

<table>
<tr><td colspan="3">harmful items, substances, etc.)</td><td colspan="3"></td></tr>
<tr><td colspan="3">One sentence to remind myself (hope + next step)</td><td colspan="3"></td></tr>
<tr><td>Week of</td><td>GAD-7 score (0–21)</td><td>Top triggers</td><td>Top safety behaviors</td><td>Approach practices completed</td><td>What I learned</td></tr>
<tr><td></td><td></td><td></td><td></td><td></td><td></td></tr>
<tr><td></td><td></td><td></td><td></td><td></td><td></td></tr>
<tr><td></td><td></td><td></td><td></td><td></td><td></td></tr>
<tr><td></td><td></td><td></td><td></td><td></td><td></td></tr>
<tr><td></td><td></td><td></td><td></td><td></td><td></td></tr>
<tr><td></td><td></td><td></td><td></td><td></td><td></td></tr>
<tr><td colspan="3">My support people (names + roles)</td><td colspan="3"></td></tr>
<tr><td colspan="3">What I'm working on (1–2 sentences)</td><td colspan="3"></td></tr>
<tr><td colspan="3">What helps me most (presence, coaching, accountability, accompaniment)</td><td colspan="3"></td></tr>
</table>

What I'm asking you NOT to do (repeated reassurance, checking for me)	
Boundary scripts we will use	
How we will review progress (weekly check-in plan)	
What to do if I'm escalating (safety plan link)	
One encouragement reminder you can say to me	
Trigger (what happened?)	
Threat story (what did anxiety predict?)	
Body alarm (what did you feel?)	
Urge (what did you want to do?)	

Safety behaviors (what did you do to reduce anxiety?)	
Short-term relief (what changed right away?)	
Long-term cost / learning (what did it teach your brain?)	
1) Situation (facts only)	
2) Automatic thought / prediction	
3) Emotion + intensity (0–100)	
4) Evidence for / evidence against	
5) Balanced thought (realistic)	
6) Next right step (action)	

Anchors at A Glance

- Anchor 1—Identity: You are not your anxiety.
- Anchor 2—Connection: Build your support team.
- Anchor 3—Awareness: Understand the anxiety loop.
- Anchor 4—Reality: Thoughts are not facts.
- Anchor 5—Approach: Move toward what you fear.
- Anchor 6—Treatment: Use evidence-based care wisely.
- Anchor 7—Body: Nervous system support matters.
- Anchor 8—Presence: Stay engaged without needing to be calm.
- Anchor 9—Being Seen: Visibility is survivable.
- Anchor 10—Boundaries: Presence helps; certainty fuels.
- Anchor 11—Consistency: Small practice beats intensity.
- Anchor 12—Maintenance: Return after setbacks.

References

Abramowitz, J. S. (2006). The psychological treatment of obsessive-compulsive disorder. Canadian Journal of Psychiatry, 51, 407–416.

American Psychiatric Association. (2022). Diagnostic and statistical manual of mental disorders (5th ed., text rev.; DSM-5-TR). American Psychiatric Publishing.

Baldwin, D. S., Waldman, S., & Allgulander, C. (2011). Evidence-based pharmacological treatment of generalized anxiety disorder. International Journal of Neuropsychopharmacology, 14(5), 697–710. https://doi.org/10.1017/S1461145710001434

Barlow, D. H. (2002). Anxiety and its disorders: The nature and treatment of anxiety and panic (2nd ed.). Guilford Press.

Bernstein, A., Hadash, Y., Lichtash, Y., Tanay, G., Shepherd, K., & Fresco, D. M. (2015). Decentering and related constructs: A critical review and metacognitive processes model. Perspectives on Psychological Science, 10(5), 599–617. https://doi.org/10.1177/1745691615594577

Clark, D. M. (1986). A cognitive approach to panic. Behaviour Research and Therapy, 24(4), 461–470. https://doi.org/10.1016/0005-7967(86)90011-2

Clark, D. M., & Wells, A. (1995). A cognitive model of social phobia. In R. G. Heimberg, M. R. Liebowitz, D. A. Hope, & F. R. Schneier (Eds.), Social phobia: Diagnosis, assessment, and treatment (pp. 69–93). Guilford Press.

Conrad, A., & Roth, W. T. (2007). Muscle relaxation therapy for anxiety disorders: It works but how? Journal of Anxiety Disorders, 21, 243–264. https://doi.org/10.1016/j.janxdis.2006.08.001

Dugas, M. J., & Robichaud, M. (2007). Cognitive-behavioral treatment for generalized anxiety disorder: From science to practice. Routledge.

Gilovich, T., Medvec, V. H., & Savitsky, K. (2000). The spotlight effect in social judgment: An egocentric bias in estimates of the salience of one's own actions and appearance. Journal of Personality and Social Psychology, 78, 211–222. https://doi.org/10.1037/0022-3514.78.2.211

Hayes, S. C., Strosahl, K. D., & Wilson, K. G. (2012). Acceptance and commitment therapy: The process and practice of mindful change (2nd ed.). Guilford Press.

Kedzior, K. K., & Laeber, L. T. (2014). A positive association between anxiety disorders and cannabis use or cannabis use disorders in the general population: A meta-analysis of 31 studies. BMC Psychiatry, 14, Article 136. https://doi.org/10.1186/1471-244X-14-136

Klevebrant, L., & Frick, A. (2022). Effects of caffeine on anxiety and panic attacks in patients with panic disorder: A systematic review and meta-analysis. General Hospital Psychiatry, 74, 22–31. https://doi.org/10.1016/j.genhosppsych.2021.11.005

Linehan, M. M. (2015). DBT skills training manual (2nd ed.). Guilford Press.

Martell, C. R., Dimidjian, S., & Herman-Dunn, R. (2010). Behavioral activation for depression: A clinician's guide. Guilford Press.

National Institute for Health and Care Excellence. (2011). Generalised anxiety disorder and panic disorder in adults: Management (CG113). https://www.nice.org.uk/guidance/cg113

National Institute of Mental Health. (n.d.). Any anxiety disorder. Retrieved January 22, 2026, from https://www.nimh.nih.gov/health/statistics/any-anxiety-disorder

Roehrs, T., & Roth, T. (2001). Sleep, sleepiness, sleep disorders and alcohol use and abuse. Sleep Medicine Reviews, 5(4), 287–297. https://doi.org/10.1053/smrv.2001.0162

Salkovskis, P. M. (1991). The importance of behaviour in the maintenance of anxiety and panic: A cognitive account. Behavioural and Cognitive Psychotherapy, 19(1), 6–19.

Spitzer, R. L., Kroenke, K., Williams, J. B. W., & Löwe, B. (2006). A brief measure for assessing generalized anxiety disorder: The GAD-7. Archives of Internal Medicine, 166(10), 1092–1097. https://doi.org/10.1001/archinte.166.10.1092

Trauer, J. M., Qian, M. Y., Doyle, J. S., Rajaratnam, S. M. W., & Cunnington, D. (2015). Cognitive behavioral therapy for chronic insomnia: A systematic review and meta-analysis. Annals of Internal Medicine, 163, 191–204. https://doi.org/10.7326/M14-2841

About the Author

Cindy H. Carr, D.Min., MACL, has spent her vocational life walking alongside people in the slow, often unseen work of formation and change. Her career has been intentionally bi-vocational, shaped by years of pastoring, business leadership, and pastoral counseling—always with a focus on helping people live with greater clarity, dignity, and wholeness.

She earned a Master of Arts in Church Leadership from Eastern Mennonite Seminary and completed her doctoral work at Liberty University. Over the years, she served multiple churches in Virginia's Shenandoah Valley in a variety of pastoral and leadership capacities.

In this season of life, Cindy's work has shifted from direct leadership into writing and education. Through her books, she helps readers implement formation-based principles she has taught throughout her career—practices centered on identity, connection, return, and steady growth without shame.

Learn more about Cindy and her work at **CindyHCarr.com**

www.ingramcontent.com/pod-product-compliance
Lightning Source LLC
LaVergne TN
LVHW011029110826
845149LV00015B/3338

9781971192277